CODING CAREERS
IN INTERNET SECURITY

Kate Shoup

New York

Published in 2020 by Cavendish Square Publishing, LLC
243 5th Avenue, Suite 136, New York, NY 10016

Copyright © 2020 by Cavendish Square Publishing, LLC

First Edition

No part of this publication may be reproduced, stored in a retrieval system, or transmitted in any form or by any means—electronic, mechanical, photocopying, recording, or otherwise—without the prior permission of the copyright owner. Request for permission should be addressed to Permissions, Cavendish Square Publishing, 243 5th Avenue, Suite 136, New York, NY 10016. Tel (877) 980-4450; fax (877) 980-4454.

Website: cavendishsq.com

This publication represents the opinions and views of the author based on his or her personal experience, knowledge, and research. The information in this book serves as a general guide only. The author and publisher have used their best efforts in preparing this book and disclaim liability rising directly or indirectly from the use and application of this book.

All websites were available and accurate when this book was sent to press.

Library of Congress Cataloging-in-Publication Data

Names: Shoup, Kate, 1972- author.
Title: Coding careers in internet security / Kate Shoup.
Description: New York : Cavendish Square, 2020. | Series: Coding careers for tomorrow | Audience: Grades 7-12. | Includes bibliographical references and index.
Identifiers: LCCN 2018059284 (print) | LCCN 2018061657 (ebook) | ISBN 9781502645838 (ebook) | ISBN 9781502645821 (library bound) | ISBN 9781502645814 (paperback)
Subjects: LCSH: Computer programming–Vocational guidance–Juvenile literature. | Computer security–Vocational guidance–Juvenile literature.
Classification: LCC QA76.6115 (ebook) | LCC QA76.6115 .S56 2020 (print) | DDC 005.8023–dc23
LC record available at https://lccn.loc.gov/2018059284

Editorial Director: David McNamara
Editor: Kristen Susienka
Copy Editor: Denise Larrabee
Associate Art Director: Alan Sliwinski
Designer: Ginny Kemmerer
Production Coordinator: Karol Szymczuk
Photo Research: J8 Media

The photographs in this book are used by permission and through the courtesy of: Cover Emir Klepo/Alamy Stock Photo; p. 1 (and used throughout the book) Maciek905/iStcockphoto.com; p. 4 ETham Photo/Getty Images; p. 6 Best-Backgrounds/Shutterstock.com; p. 8 Digital Vision/Getty Images; p. 10 Mary Holzer & Matt Crypto/Wikimedia Commons/File:Diffie and Hellman.jpg/CC BY-SA-3.0, (used throughout) MF3d/iStockphoto.com; p. 12 Aleksandar Nakic/Getty Images; p. 14 Miguel Candela/SOPA Images/LightRocket/Getty Images; p. 18 Michael J. Okoniewski/AP Photo; p. 24 Richard Ellis/Alamy Stock Photo; p. 27 Sundry Photography/Shutterstock.com; p. 28 Bangoland/Shutterstock.com; p. 30 Monsitj/iStock/Getty Images; p. 33 Matejmo/iStock/Getty Images; p. 37 Charles Brutlag/Shutterstock.com; p. 39 Izabela Habur/Getty Images; p. 42 Gerald Herbert/AP Photo; p. 44 Time Stopper/Getty Images; p. 50 J.M. Eddins Jr./Air Force Photo; p. 51 Grinvalds/iStock/Getty Images; p. 54 Daniel Acker/Bloomberg/Getty Images; p. 56 South Agency/Getty Images; p. 61 Corey Williams/AP Photo; p. 62 Sol Stock/iStock/Getty Images; p. 63 David Becker/Bloomberg/Getty Images; p. 64 NSF; p. 66 NASA.

Printed in the United States of America

Contents

chapter_01 An Introduction to Coding in Internet Security 5

chapter_02 How Coders Have Improved Internet Security 15

chapter_03 Coding to Combat Cybercrime 31

chapter_04 Jobs in Internet Security 45

chapter_05 Getting Involved 57

Glossary 69

Further Information 72

Selected Bibliography 74

Index 78

About the Author 80

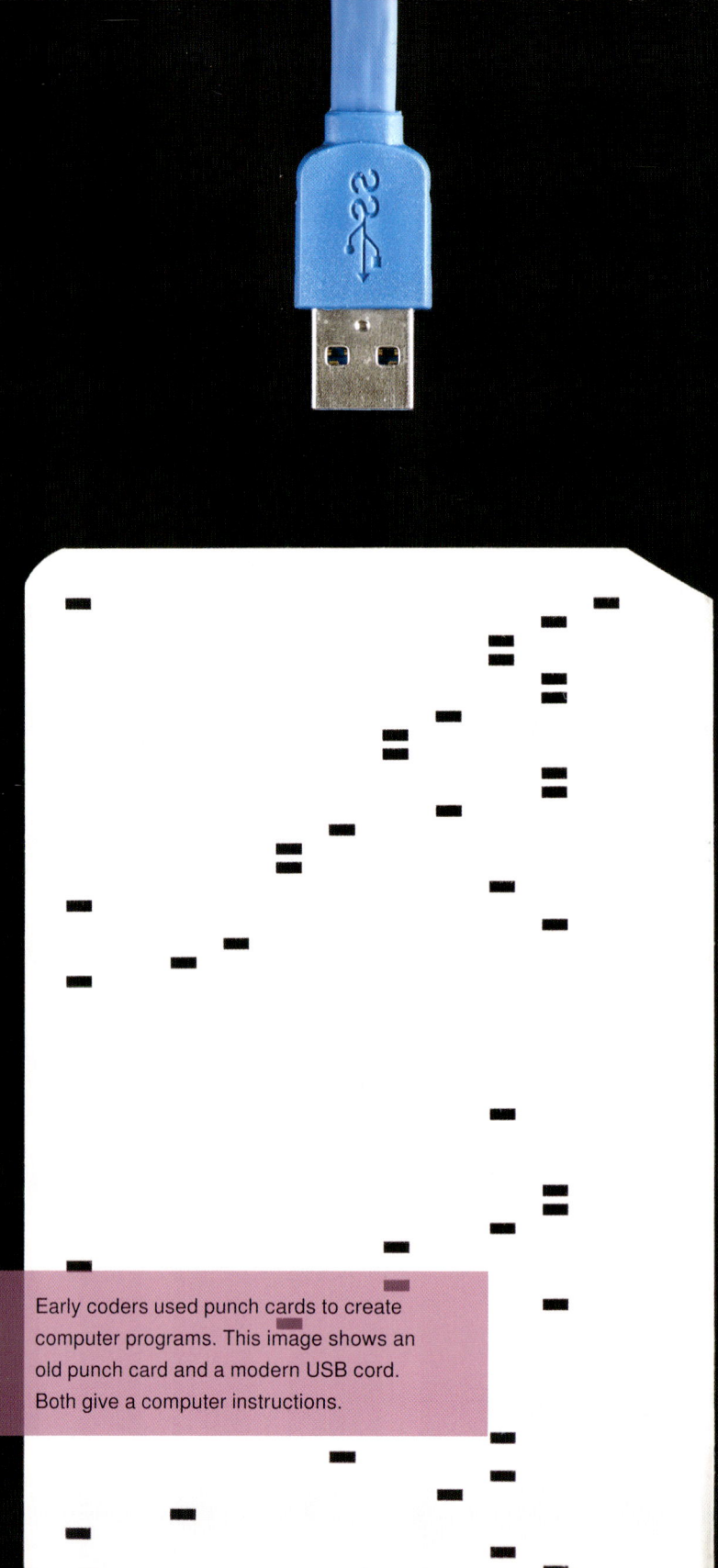

Early coders used punch cards to create computer programs. This image shows an old punch card and a modern USB cord. Both give a computer instructions.

chapter_01

An Introduction to Coding in Internet Security

Computer coding is the process of designing and building a computer program to perform a particular set of tasks. This process is also called computer programming or software development. Early computer coders used punch cards to build computer programs. It worked like this: a coder wrote out the data and program instructions for the program. The coder (or a helper) then punched holes into a card in a set pattern for each piece of data or program instruction. There might be hundreds or even thousands of these cards for a given program. The complete set of cards for a program was called the source deck. The source deck was fed into a machine called a compiler. The compiler converted the program instructions into a special language called machine language and produced a new stack of cards with holes punched through them called the program deck. This was the program. A computer operator could insert a program deck into a computer to perform the task the program was built to complete.

COMPUTER CODING AS A CORE COMPETENCY

Today, coders build programs by typing program instructions into a computer text file. These instructions are called source code. Program instructions are written in one of several programming languages. In most cases, coders feed the source code into a computer program called a compiler. The compiler converts the source code into a program. There are

Here is an example of modern computer code.

[6] Coding Careers in Internet Security

literally millions of computer programs designed to perform all sorts of tasks.

Computer coding used to be a special skill that few people knew how to do. Today, it is a core competency for young people—like reading, writing, or math. This is because more and more jobs require computer-coding skills.

COMPUTER CODING AND INTERNET SECURITY

Computer coders work in many different industries. Some work in health care. Others work in manufacturing, communications, or transportation. Still others work in the military or in government agencies. Some computer coders specialize in an area called internet security or cybersecurity. A US Department of Defense division called the Advanced Research Projects Agency (ARPA) developed the internet during the 1960s—except they called it the ARPANET. At first, the ARPANET consisted of only four linked computers—three in California and one in Utah. Today, the internet connects billions of computers around the globe.

The importance of the internet cannot be overstated. "As a nation, we are dependent on the internet," says the US National Security Agency (NSA). Businesses and other organizations, including government agencies, use the internet constantly. And every day, people use the network to shop, bank, and communicate. "We all count on having

Today, coders can find jobs in many places. Some internet security jobs are found at the Pentagon.

ready access to the internet and its many capabilities," says the NSA.

This makes the internet particularly attractive to hackers. Hackers are computer users who break into a computer system, usually to steal personal information stored on a computer.

Some hackers are motivated by profit. Their goal is often to steal personal data from computer users and use this information to apply for credit cards or loans. This practice is called identity theft. They achieve this by breaking into business systems to steal customer data or by accessing the machines of individual users to search for sensitive information. Hackers who do this are often called cybercriminals.

Other hackers want to create chaos. They often do this by infecting computer systems with programs called malware. Malware is short for malicious software. It is a type of computer program built by hackers whose purpose is to damage or exploit a computer system in some way. Malware attacks can be very damaging. For example, a cybercriminal could hurt the economy by attacking business systems. Or a cybercriminal could shut down the electrical grid by attacking a power company's computer systems. Both scenarios could result in serious social unrest!

Then there are the hackers who have a more nationalistic aim. These hackers might breach a computer system of a foreign government to gain insight into military activities or foreign policy. They might even shut down a government computer system as an act of war. These hackers are often called cyberterrorists.

Computer coders who specialize in internet security can help prevent these types of cyberattacks. These cybersecurity professionals make the internet—and the world—safer.

CODING JOBS IN INTERNET SECURITY

Coders who specialize in internet security have several job options available to them. One of these positions is a security software developer. A security software developer builds programs that secure computer systems against cyberattacks.

PUBLIC KEY ENCRYPTION

Whitfield Diffie (*left*) and Martin Hellman (*right*) were some of the first pioneers of encryption.

Encryption is an important weapon against hackers. It is a way of protecting information by scrambling it. Many computer systems use a method called public key encryption to protect private communications. This method was developed during the 1970s by a professor of electrical engineering at Stanford University named Martin Hellman and a graduate student named Whitfield Diffie.

Before Hellman and Diffie, only the US government used encryption. In fact, the NSA discouraged the study of encryption by academics. The *New York Times* reported, "There was very little published material about modern methods [of encryption] and much was classified."

Despite this, Hellman and Diffie began work on their own encryption system in 1974. By 1976, they had made what became known as the Diffie-Hellman key exchange—one of the first public key encryption protocols. This system was both simple and almost impossible to crack. It allowed people to safely communicate over a network with total privacy. After its release, the NSA threatened to prosecute Hellman and Diffie, but eventually let it go.

Without Hellman, Diffie, and other computer scientists interested in encryption, the internet might never have taken hold. Certainly, common online activities like shopping and banking would be impossible. Thanks to Diffie and Hellman's work, "the Internet has become a place of commerce and communication" and is "a safe place to exchange goods and services," says *Wired* magazine.

An example of a security program is an anti-malware program. Anti-malware programs prevent malware from entering a computer system. Anti-malware programs also scan computer systems to detect and delete any malware that may have sneaked through.

Another job for coders who specialize in internet security is a cryptographer. A cryptographer develops ciphers, or codes, to encrypt sensitive information on a computer system. That way, even if a hacker successfully breaks into a computer

Coders who specialize in internet security have all sorts of job options! This woman is scrolling through code at her job.

[12]   Coding Careers in Internet Security

system, that person can't read the information stored there. Some cryptographers work for government agencies like the NSA or the Central Intelligence Agency (CIA).

A third job in internet security is working as a penetration tester, or white-hat hacker. A penetration tester breaks into a computer system the same way a hacker does. The difference is that the penetration tester does it to help an organization find security flaws in their computer systems—not to steal information from or damage those systems. This practice is called ethical hacking.

These are just three of the jobs available to coders who specialize in internet security. However, there are many more to choose from and explore.

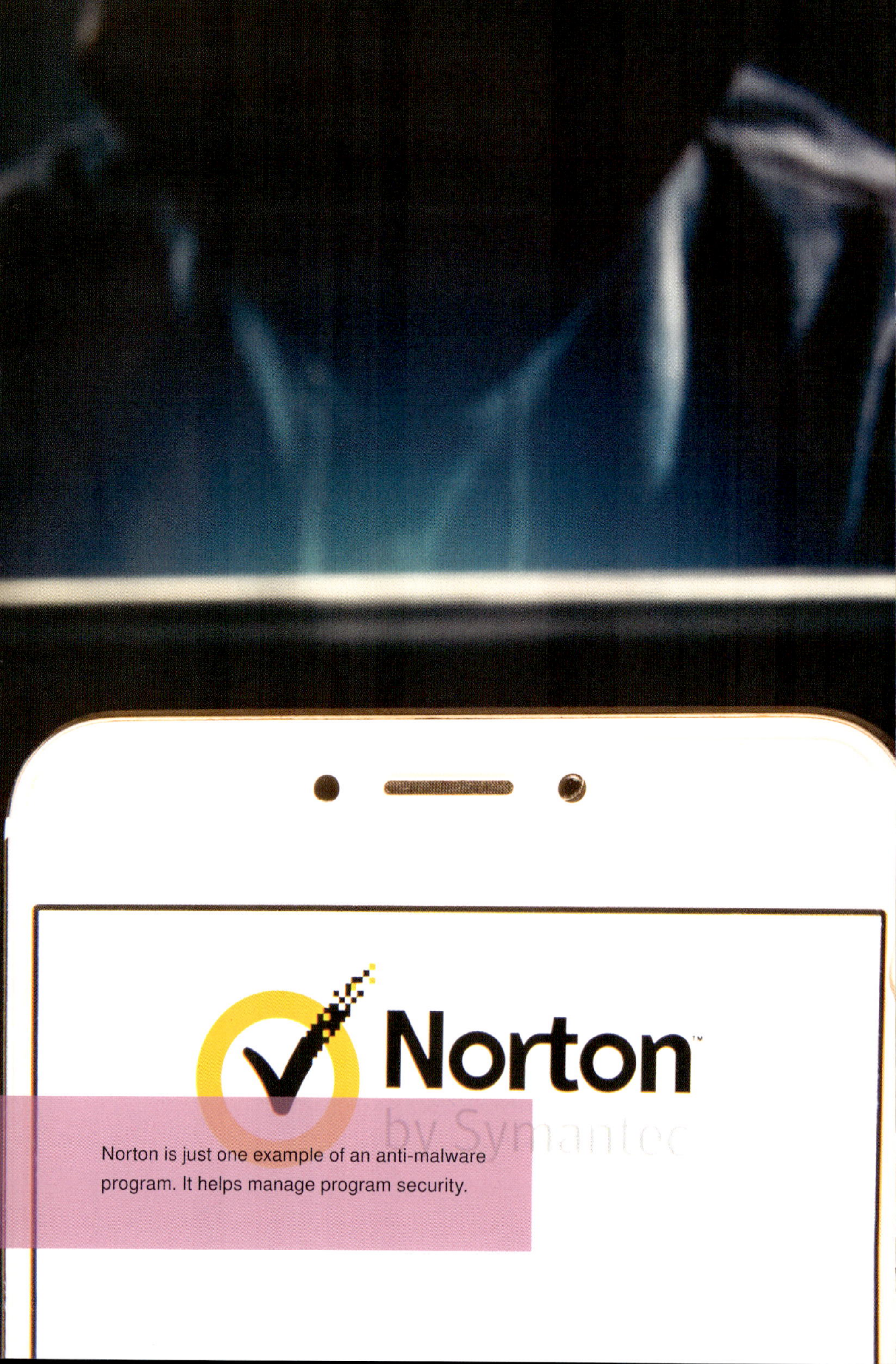

Norton is just one example of an anti-malware program. It helps manage program security.

Coding Careers in Internet Security

chapter_02

How Coders Have Improved Internet Security

Computer coders improve internet security in two main ways. One is by building software to block malware. The other is by designing computer systems with minimal security flaws to prevent malware or hackers from accessing these systems. In both cases, malware is the chief threat.

THE THREAT OF MALWARE

There are several types of malware. Some are merely annoying. Others are extremely dangerous. On the annoying end is adware. Adware causes pop-up advertisements to appear on a user's screen. A more dangerous type is spyware. Spyware can scan a system for personal information, track the user's internet activity, and detect what the user types on the keyboard—including the usernames and passwords the user employs to access various internet accounts. Other dangerous types of malware change or erase system files; wreck the system's hard drive; or create another way into the system, which a hacker can use to take it over completely. Then there's ransomware. It locks down a system until the user pays a ransom.

Some varieties of malware have a different purpose altogether: to disable computer systems. These are called viruses and worms. Much like a biological virus attaches itself to a living host, a computer virus attaches itself to a program or file on a computer system. When the host program or file is run, the virus makes a copy of itself. The copy then attaches itself to another program or file. When that program or file runs, the malware self-replicates again, and so on, until the system contains so many copies of the virus it runs out of resources to handle them all. Like a virus, a worm spreads by self-replicating. However, unlike a virus, which requires a program or file to be run in order to spread, a worm can spread all on its own.

Malware generally infects a computer system using one of two methods. One method involves detecting security flaws in a computer system and using these flaws to access it. Security flaws are usually the result of bugs. A bug is an error or flaw in a computer system or program (usually in its source code) that causes it to behave in an unintended way. This often opens a pathway for malware to exploit the system. Malware that uses a security flaw to infect a computer system is sometimes called a zero-day exploit.

The second malware-infection method is a mechanism called a Trojan horse, or Trojan. Hackers spread Trojan horses by tricking users into installing them. Some Trojans pose as a harmless or even useful program; its malicious nature is revealed only when the user installs it. Other Trojans are spread via email messages. These messages warn users of some type of problem and instruct them to click a link in the message to find out more. Of course, when the user clicks the link, they download the Trojan. This tactic is called phishing.

Malware is a serious problem. Anti-malware maker Kaspersky Lab detected more than fifteen million pieces of malicious code in 2017, affecting nearly 30 percent of computers. Experts predict that annual financial losses due to malware and other types of cybercrime will hit $6 trillion by 2021. It's up to computer coders who specialize in internet security to stop the criminals who make malware.

EARLY EXAMPLES OF MALWARE ATTACKS

Most early forms of malware weren't meant to damage or exploit computer systems. Instead, they were the products of experiments by computer coders.

In 1971, computer coders developed a worm called Creeper as an experiment. It was meant to show how a computer program could self-replicate and move from one computer to another on a network. Creeper did not damage the computers it infected. It simply displayed a message to the user.

Another example of an experiment was the Morris worm. A young computer coder named Robert Morris built the worm to highlight security flaws in the ARPANET. However, a problem in its code caused the worm to cripple the network.

Creeper and the Morris worm had no malicious intent (even though the Morris worm did cause damage). This was

Robert Morris built one of the first pieces of malware ever. It was called the Morris worm.

not so with another malware program unleashed in 1974, called the Rabbit (or Wabbit) virus. This virus was designed to quickly self-replicate on a computer system until the machine became bogged down and crashed. Another malware program unleashed in 1986 also had malicious intent. The hackers who built this program disguised it as an updated version of a popular, free word-processing program called PC-Write. When users installed the program on their machine, it deleted all the files on their system. This program was the first known Trojan.

These early examples of malware were effective. However, they did not cause widespread damage. There were three main reasons for this. First, few people owned personal computers (PCs) at that time. Second, few organizations had computer networks. Third, the internet (or, more precisely, the ARPANET) was used mainly by government officials and academics.

That changed in the 1990s. It was during this period that companies began building and selling PCs to regular consumers, computer networks became more popular among businesses and other organizations, and the internet and related software like web browsers and email programs became available for the public to use.

As more people got online, email quickly became a popular way for hackers to spread malware. One example of this was the Melissa virus that swept the internet in 1999. It worked like this: A computer user received an email message with a Microsoft Word document attached. When the user opened the document, it infected the person's computer with the virus. The virus then scanned the infected system to determine whether it had the Microsoft Outlook email program installed. If so, the virus located the Outlook email address book and forwarded itself to fifty of the user's contacts. Although the Melissa virus didn't exactly damage the infected computer, it did generate lots of network traffic—so much that it caused many networks to crash.

One year later, another malware program, called the I Love You virus, caused even more problems. It acted exactly like the Melissa virus, except that instead of forwarding itself to the first fifty contacts in an infected machine's Outlook address book, it forwarded itself to everyone—and also deleted random files. The I Love You virus quickly infected an estimated fifty million machines and caused between $5 and $15 billion worth of damages worldwide.

MODERN MALWARE ATTACKS

The twenty-first century has seen more damaging malware attacks. One of these occurred in 2017. This attack used a malware program called WannaCry. It exploited a security flaw in certain versions of the Microsoft Windows operating system to lock down computers worldwide. The hackers behind this attack demanded that affected users pay a ransom to retrieve their data or lose it forever. Fortunately, Microsoft quickly issued a patch for the security flaw. A patch is a piece of code meant to fix, or patch up, a security flaw in an operating system or other computer program. Software makers distribute patches by releasing updates to their software. More important, security experts also discovered a kill switch in the malware program to stop it from spreading. This helped limit the number of computers affected and the damage done—although it was still significant.

Another 2017 malware attack called NotPetya proved far more destructive. NotPetya exploited the same security flaw as WannaCry but lacked a kill switch. NotPetya was designed to spread quickly. One security expert called it "simply the fastest propagating piece of malware we've ever seen." But that's not all. After NotPetya infected a system, it worked extremely quickly to disable it. It took down the entire network of a large bank in Ukraine in just forty-five seconds! At first, it seemed that NotPetya was ransomware like WannaCry. It even displayed a screen demanding a ransom payment. However, soon it became clear to investigators that its purpose was to permanently destroy the contents of every system it infected. Investigators also discovered that it had likely been unleashed by Russia as an act of cyber war against Ukraine and its allies—opening a "new era of warfare" that involves "undermining democracy, wrecking livelihoods by targeting critical infrastructure and weaponizing information," said British defense secretary Gavin Williamson.

As discussed, not all malware attacks involve destroying computer systems. Some hackers craft malware with another aim: to steal the data on a compromised system. This might include private customer information, trade secrets on a business system, or classified information on a government system. In one incident in 2016, a group of hackers called the Shadow Brokers accessed machines maintained by the US National Security Agency—the organization responsible for ensuring cybersecurity in the United States. The Shadow Brokers then stole top-secret hacking tools that the agency had developed and released them on the dark web. The dark web is a corner of the internet that allows for completely anonymous communications and mostly traffics in illegal goods, including malware. These tools could "undermine the security of a lot of major government and corporate networks both here and abroad," said one security expert.

A new type of malware attack is called crypto-jacking. This involves infecting machines with malware that secretly "mines" digital money, called crypto currency. When someone spends crypto currency, the transaction is entered into a secure ledger called a blockchain. The blockchain approves transactions using a complex algorithm—an operation that requires lots of processing power. To increase the processing power available to the blockchain, people can connect their computers to it in exchange for a small payment issued in crypto currency. This practice is called crypto-mining. So, with crypto-jacking, malware installed on a user's machine connects the machine to the blockchain—but sends the payment to the hacker who installed it. This can be quite profitable if the hacker infects enough machines.

These are just a few examples of recent malware attacks. There have been millions of others. In fact, chances are, thousands of attacks are happening right now.

THE DANGERS OF BUGS

Malware poses the most serious threat to security. But it isn't the only one. Other threats stem from computer bugs, or problems.

Some bugs open pathways for malware to enter a system. However, others create different security problems. One example was the Y2K bug in 1999. Early coders frequently used two digits to represent a year (for example, 06/17/88) instead of four (06/17/1988). As the year 2000 (commonly called Y2K) approached, people worried that computers might interpret two-digit year entries in computer code incorrectly. For example, they thought computers might translate the date 01/01/00 to January 1, 1900. They feared that this would cause some computers and networks to crash. Experts warned that if this were to happen to computer systems that managed air traffic or the power grid, the results

US president Bill Clinton delivers a speech about Y2K in 1998.

could be catastrophic. Some people even predicted it would cause a complete breakdown of society, or even bring about the end of the world. Fortunately, thanks to feverish (and costly) efforts by computer coders to fix the bug in systems worldwide, its effects were minimal.

EARLY EFFORTS TO SECURE THE INTERNET

Early computer users gave little thought to internet security. This was because few people used the internet or understood how it could be abused.

The release of the Creeper worm in 1971 gave an early clue to potential security problems on the internet. It also resulted in what's believed to be the first example of an anti-malware program, Reaper. Reaper was built by the same computer coders who released Creeper. It moved from machine to machine to find and delete all instances of Creeper on the network. (Interestingly, Reaper was technically a virus, but it was one designed for good.)

As malware became more complex and advanced, so did the anti-malware tools to fight it. Many of these were built by coders working for internet security companies in the late 1980s. Several security companies that still exist today started during this period. These include Symantec, Sophos, McAfee, Avast, and Panda Security. All of these companies employed (and continue to employ) computer coders to combat cybercrime.

Around the same time, informal groups of coders formed to combat malware. One of these was an online group called VIRUS-L. It started in 1988. Its members—which included some of the biggest names in internet security today, like Eugene Kaspersky, who started Kaspersky Lab in 1997—discussed new viruses and possible ways to detect and eliminate them. More formal groups like the Computer Antivirus Research Organization (CARO) and the European Institute for Computer Antivirus Research (EICAR) started to

CONTRIBUTIONS OF COMPUTER CODERS TO SECURE INTERNET SHOPPING

Before the 1990s, people usually bought items at stores near to where they lived. If the item they needed or wanted wasn't available, they might be able to order it from a printed catalog. However, more often they just went without and found something else to fill their need.

The internet changed all that. During the mid-1990s, entrepreneurs launched e-commerce sites, where people could buy and sell items online. Thanks to sites like Amazon and eBay (which both launched in 1995), it became possible to research, locate, and buy just about anything from just about anywhere—often for less money.

None of this would have been possible without computer coders who specialized in internet security. These coders

Amazon was among the first major e-commerce sites ever created.

developed tools to allow secure connections between buyers and sellers. This prevented hackers from intercepting payment information such as credit card numbers. Without secure connections, electronic financial transactions of any kind would be impossible. So, the next time you buy something online, thank a computer coder!

conduct further research into malware, and other security topics soon followed.

INTERNET SECURITY TODAY

Advancements in technology bring new challenges for computer coders who specialize in internet security. For example, innovations like mobile technologies, cloud computing, and the Internet of Things have created new attack venues for hackers. It's up to security coders to manage these threats—while at the same time fend off attacks on more traditional targets.

It won't be enough to simply respond to attacks. As members of a society that is increasingly connected and reliant on technology, internet security specialists will need to be proactive—anticipating attacks and preventing them before they occur. Only by preemptively blocking threats before they do damage can the "good guys" win.

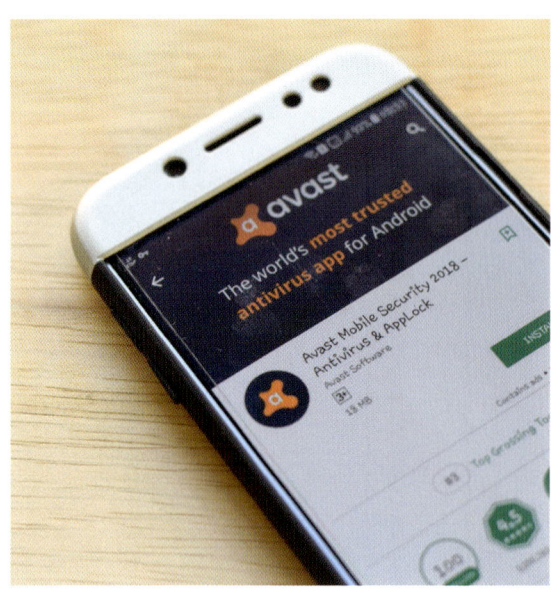

Today, anti-malware programs are helping to keep technology like cell phones virus-free.

[28]   Coding Careers in Internet Security

THE INTERNET SECURITY ARMS RACE

Each time a "bad" computer coder unleashes a new malware program on the internet, "good" computer coders quickly respond with an antidote. Without these good coders to help combat malware, the internet and the millions of computers that connect to it would likely cease to operate.

However, there's a downside: this constant back and forth has devolved into an arms race of sorts. With each attack and counterattack, an escalation occurs. Bad coders release even more destructive malware for an even greater impact.

This challenge is further complicated by the fact that making and distributing malware can be very profitable. According to Carbon Black, a cybersecurity company, some malware makers make more than $100,000 a year selling their software on the dark web—compared to $69,000 a year on average for legitimate software developers. The Federal Bureau of Investigation (FBI) estimated that in 2016 hackers collected $1 billion alone in payments to unlock ransomware.

"There's a bad-guy industry," says one security expert. "It's very profitable." So, "the good-guy industry has to be better than they are." That's the challenge for good coders who specialize in internet security: to be better than the bad coders who build malware.

Often, malware programs have a sort of "digital fingerprint."

Coding Careers in Internet Security

chapter_03

Coding to Combat Cybercrime

In 1987, a famous computer scientist named Fred Cohen observed that "there is no algorithm that can perfectly detect all possible computer viruses." A computer algorithm is an equation or a series of steps that allows a computer to complete a task or solve a problem. Cohen was correct. This explains why anti-malware programs approach detecting and destroying malware differently.

TRADITIONAL MALWARE-DETECTION STRATEGIES

Most traditional anti-malware programs identify malware by searching for signatures in computer files or transmissions. A signature is a string of information in a piece of code that

Coding to Combat Cybercrime   [31]

can be used to identify the code—like a fingerprint. Many malware programs have distinct signatures. When an anti-malware program detects one of these signatures, it knows to delete the code.

To prevent anti-malware software from detecting signatures, some hackers encrypt their code. This is called obfuscation. Before the encrypted code can run on the target machine, however, it must be decrypted. Often the code used to decrypt the malicious code—called a decryptor—has a signature all its own. So, although anti-malware software might not be able to detect the signature of the encrypted code, it can sometimes detect the signature of a decryptor.

As a counterattack, hackers developed new methods to encrypt and decrypt malware. One of these methods involves the use of oligomorphic code. Oligomorphic code includes multiple decryptors, each one capable of decrypting the malware. When the malware runs, it chooses one of these decryptors at random. Having multiple decryptors makes it harder for anti-malware software to detect a signature.

Other methods include polymorphic code and metamorphic code. With both these types of code, the decryptor mutates as the code runs (although in slightly different ways). This makes it almost impossible for anti-malware programs to detect their signatures—which means new detection methods are needed.

NEXT-GENERATION MALWARE-DETECTION METHODS

In the twenty-first century, coders who specialize in internet security have developed several new methods to detect malware. These are often described as next-generation methods.

One next-generation method is generic decryption. With generic decryption the anti-malware program loads all new program files into an emulator. An emulator is like a second virtual computer inside the same physical machine as a "regular" computer but isolated from the regular computer's hard drive and other key resources. The emulator scans and runs each new program to detect malware signatures, or behaviors that are consistent with malware. If the emulator determines that the program is malware, it shuts it down and deletes it. Because the emulator is isolated from the regular

Encryption in some messages is an important tool.

computer (even though they're in the same physical machine) the malware cannot spread.

Some types of anti-malware programs take a similar approach but load new programs in a sandbox in the cloud rather than in an emulator on the user's computer. A sandbox is an isolated virtual space for testing software. The cloud refers to computers on the internet that host software and services. Users can connect to the cloud to run software or services from those computers rather than from their own.

Other next-generation methods use technologies like machine learning (ML). Machine learning involves developing algorithms or models to allow machines to learn over time. Coders include machine learning models in their anti-malware programs to detect malware that uses polymorphic or metamorphic code. These models detect malware by noticing when a program contains unusual code or behaves in a suspicious way. Machine learning can also help identify the person or group who made a piece of malware by identifying certain patterns in the code, giving law enforcement officials help in the fight against cybercrime.

Not surprisingly, hackers have also begun using machine learning. Sometimes they use it to build sneakier malware programs. Other times they design it to trick or confuse machine learning models used by anti-malware programs and cause them to make mistakes. This is called adversarial machine learning.

COMMON CODING LANGUAGES

Coders build computer programs (including malware and anti-malware) by typing program instructions written using a programming language into a computer file. These program instructions are called source code. Most source code is run through a special computer program called a compiler. The compiler translates the programming language in the source code into a machine language that a computer can read. (Some source code is designed to skip this step. This code is said to be interpreted.) Machine language consists of a series of zeroes and ones. The order in which these zeroes and ones appear dictates how the program will behave. The code that contains this machine language is called object code.

There are literally thousands of programming languages. Different programming languages have different characteristics. Some programming languages are low-level languages. This means they are similar to machine language. They are harder for humans to read and learn. Others are high-level. This means they often use elements of human language (like words), have a set structure, and may automate certain programming functions. This makes them easier to learn and use. Other characteristics of a programming language include whether it has a generic purpose or a specific use; whether it is imperative (containing a sequence of specific operations to perform to achieve a desired outcome) or declarative

More on Machine Learning

Many people use the terms artificial intelligence (AI) and machine learning interchangeably. However, they are not quite the same thing. Artificial intelligence refers to the science and engineering behind so-called intelligent machines. An example of a machine that uses AI is Amazon's digital personal assistant, Alexa. Another example are the chatbots used for customer service on some websites. In contrast, machine learning describes the ability of machines to learn through experience over time. So, machine learning is a way to achieve artificial intelligence.

Machine learning represents the cutting edge of cybersecurity. It also embodies the strongest defense against malware—especially when used with other security methods like scanning for signatures in an emulator or on the cloud. Machine learning is uniquely suited for the work associated

Amazon's Alexa uses artificial intelligence to communicate and perform requests from users.

with combating malware—quickly performing routine tasks (such as scanning files) and handling huge amounts of data (to identify and categorize the millions of strains of malware on the internet). It does this work more quickly and effectively than a human ever could!

Coding to Combat Cybercrime [37]

(specifying the desired result but not the steps needed to achieve it); and so on.

Coders who specialize in internet security need not study every programming language. This would be impossible. But there are a few they should learn. These include the following:

- JavaScript: JavaScript is an interpreted, imperative, high-level programming language. It is frequently used to build interactive web pages and appears in the source code for most modern websites. It's among the most widely used programming languages.

- HTML: Virtually all websites include HTML code. It's therefore important for coders who specialize in internet security to know HTML. This language is very easy to learn.

- Python: Like JavaScript, Python is an interpreted, imperative, high-level programming language. Like HTML, it's easy to learn. Python mimics human language. This makes it very popular among less-experienced malware makers.

- C and C++: C was developed during the 1970s and remains a popular general-purpose programming language. C is considered a high-level language—but not as high-level as some others, such as Python. C++ is an updated version of C. It compiles more quickly and provides better overall performance.

There are a few programming languages that students interested in specializing in internet security should learn. Here, students are learning different programming techniques.

THE MOVEMENT TO OPEN SOURCE CODE

In the late 1990s, some software developers began moving from building proprietary software (which is owned by a specific person or organization) to using an open source model. Open source software's source code is available to the general public to study or even modify. Since its development, open source software has become quite popular. This kind of software development encourages collaboration. Because more people review and modify open source code, it is almost always stronger and more secure than proprietary code. For

Coding to Combat Cybercrime [39]

example, the Linux operating system, which is open source, is more secure than both the Windows and MacOS operating systems, which are proprietary.

The open source model is particularly well suited for the area of internet security. The practice of using open source software in this context is called open security. According to open source advocate David A. Wheeler, open security is effective because "defenders working together to eliminate and remediate vulnerabilities are likely to be far more effective than if they work in isolation." In addition to collaborating to make software more secure, "defenders" can also unite to build more effective anti-malware programs. As security expert Kevin Keeney explains, to combat "today's increasingly wily cyber adversary," coders "need to be moving in the direction of open source projects that enable us to collaborate and fight as a team."

One organization devoted to the promotion of open source code is the Open Web Application Security Project (OWASP). In its own words, OWASP is a "worldwide not-for-profit charitable organization focused on improving the security of software." This nonprofit organization distributes reading materials and tools to help people who want to use the open source approach to improve the security of their computer programs. (For more information, see https://www.owasp.org.)

LEGISLATIVE AND GOVERNMENTAL EFFORTS TO STOP HACKERS

Creating secure programs and building anti-malware software are two ways to combat cybercrime. A third way is to pass laws to deter hackers.

American lawmakers introduced the first law to combat computer crime in 1977. This law was called the Federal Computer Systems Protection Act. However, this law did not pass—perhaps because lawmakers lacked an understanding of computers and how they might be used for criminal purposes.

In 1983, a top FBI agent testified in Congress that a computer could be used in much the same way as "a gun, a knife, or a forger's pen" to commit a crime. This testimony helped prompt the passage of the Computer Fraud and Abuse Act of 1984—the first US federal law to fight computer crime. Since then, US lawmakers have passed several more cybercrime laws.

To enforce cybercrime laws and improve cybersecurity, the US government has created several divisions within key government agencies. These include the Computer Emergency Response Team, the Office of Cybersecurity and Communications, the Cyber Crimes Center, the National Cyber Investigative Joint Task Force, the National Security Cyber Specialist network, and the National Security Cyber

Assistance Program, to name a few. Many of these government divisions hire computer coders to help stop hackers.

US cybersecurity laws largely deal with criminal acts against organizations. They do not dictate whether or how organizations protect their computer systems or networks against attack. This is unfortunate. The failure of an organization to properly secure its systems can have grave consequences for everyday Americans if their data is stolen by hackers. However, one US government agency, the National Institute of Standards and Technology (NIST), has developed guidelines for securing computer systems. These guidelines are called the NIST Cybersecurity Framework. They are

The FBI is just one government agency that hires coders who specialize in internet security. Here, an FBI agent works in a computer forensics lab.

Coding Careers in Internet Security

designed to help businesses and other organizations prevent and protect against cyberattacks, detect cyberattacks, and respond to and recover from cyberattacks.

The European Union (EU), a group of countries in Europe working together, has taken a much stricter approach to ensuring the security of computer systems and networks. In 2016 it passed a law called the General Data Protection Regulation (GDPR). This law requires companies that collect private customer data to explain in simple terms how they handle it. The law also requires companies to take reasonable steps to protect private data and to report a data breach within a prescribed period of time. It's important for coders who specialize in internet security to be aware of these laws (or lack thereof)—especially coders whose job is to secure applications and networks that host private data.

Hackers are constantly trying to break into secure places online. This perpetuates the need for internet security experts.

Coding Careers in Internet Security

chapter_04

Jobs in Internet Security

There is much need for computer coders in the twenty-first century. The US Bureau of Labor Statistics has predicted a 24 percent increase in the number of computer-coding jobs between 2016 and 2026. The median salary for these jobs is more than $100,000 per year—well above the national average salary. It's no wonder *US News & World Report* ranked software developer as the number one best job in the United States in 2018!

AN INCREASING DEMAND FOR CYBERSECURITY CODERS

If coders are highly sought-after, coders who specialize in internet security are even more desired. There are various reasons for this. One reason is that cybercrime is increasing. In 2010, there were 3.8 million recorded security breaches. In 2016, there were almost one hundred times that many breaches, 3.1 billion. It seems extremely likely the number of breaches will continue to grow. Another reason coders are highly sought after is that hackers are releasing more and more types of malware. As noted earlier, Kaspersky Lab detected more than fifteen million pieces of malicious code in 2017. Much of this malware is relatively unsophisticated—the work of young hackers and other amateurs. However, some of it is very complex—not to mention dangerous.

Finally, there just aren't enough cybersecurity specialists to go around. According to a 2018 report released by the Information Systems Audit and Control Association (ISACA), more than half of all organizations say it takes at least three months to fill open cybersecurity positions—and more than one-quarter of organizations say they are unable to fill these positions at all. In the coming years this shortage is likely to increase unless more people join the field. Experts predict that by 2022 there will be 1.8 million more cybersecurity jobs than there are cybersecurity professionals to fill them.

The US federal government is expected to be hardest hit by this shortage of cybersecurity professionals. This will put the nation at greater risk of cyberattack. As one security expert put it, "The greatest virtual threat today is not state-sponsored cyberattacks, newfangled clandestine malware, or a hacker culture run amok. The most dangerous looming crisis … is instead a severe cybersecurity labor shortage."

Simply put, young people who are interested in specializing in internet security will have many opportunities to succeed!

JOBS IN INTERNET SECURITY

While three jobs in internet security have already been mentioned—security software developer, cryptographer, and penetration tester—there are many other opportunities out there. Some other cybersecurity jobs involve building secure computer systems and networks. Examples of these jobs are security architect and security engineer. A security architect decides which approach an organization will take to protect its computer systems. He or she then designs and implements a framework to achieve protection. As for building and maintaining this framework, a security engineer does that job.

Other jobs in internet security pertain to assessing and maintaining the security of existing systems. Examples of these jobs include security analyst and security specialist. People in these positions perform a variety of tasks to assess and maintain the security of a system, such as conducting audits and implementing security measures. Some of these tasks could involve coding, while others might not.

Security audits are conducted by security auditors and vulnerability assessors. People in these roles identify security flaws in a system or network—not by breaking into a system the way a penetration tester does, but by examining the system and using their knowledge of common security flaws to identify possible weaknesses. In a similar vein, a source code assessor scours the source code behind an organization's computer systems for bugs or other security weaknesses.

Progressing up the career ladder are jobs like security manager, security director, and chief information security officer (CISO). People in these jobs focus more on developing security strategies and managing others than on using their own coding skills.

For organizations that employ people to fill all these roles, a cyberattack or security breach is less likely but not unheard of. That's where incident responders and forensic experts come in. Incident responders (also called intrusion analysts) are like cyber firefighters. Their job is to put out the fire when a security incident occurs. Forensic experts are digital detectives. They gather and analyze the electronic evidence on computer systems, networks, and devices after an attack to identify the attack's type and source. Some forensic experts work within large organizations. Others are on the payroll of government or law enforcement agencies.

INDUSTRIES ASSOCIATED WITH INTERNET SECURITY

Coders who specialize in internet security work in many industries. These include the government, health care, manufacturing, retail, and banking.

Working in internet security for the government can be particularly gratifying. For one thing, these government jobs are usually stable. That means people aren't likely to lose their jobs. They also offer good benefits and on-the-job training. Plus, these jobs give cybersecurity experts an opportunity to serve their country. However, pay for government and military positions may be less than for comparable positions in businesses or organizations outside the government.

Several US agencies employ cybersecurity professionals. These include the NSA, the CIA, the Department of Homeland Security (DHS), and the FBI. Cybersecurity professionals also work in the four major military branches: the US Air Force, the US Army, the US Marine Corps, and the US Navy. In addition to these, several businesses that do contract work for the US government employ cybersecurity professionals. These include companies like General Dynamics, Booz Allen Hamilton, Raytheon, and Endgame, Inc.

Given the shortage of cybersecurity professionals in the federal government, these agencies are eager to hire

The US military has lots of jobs for coders who specialize in internet security—and will even train them on the job.

people. According to the DHS website, one of its "highest priorities is to acquire, grow, and sustain the most talented people in cybersecurity." This does not mean they hire everyone, however. Most jobs require the applicant to pass a background check. Some even require a security clearance. A security clearance gives the holder access to confidential or even classified information.

Another industry with a growing need for cybersecurity professionals is health care. In fact, today, the health-care industry is the most targeted industry among hackers. The main reason for this is that more and more health-care providers have begun using electronic medical records. These records contain information about a patient's health as well as identifying information such as their name, address, birthdate, and Social Security number. According to one security expert, these records "are a treasure trove of personally identifiable information that makes health-care institutions and their partners irresistible targets for cybercriminals." Hackers typically target electronic medical records to steal a patient's identity. But hackers could also alter these records to physically harm patients—for example, by changing the ordered dose of a prescription drug.

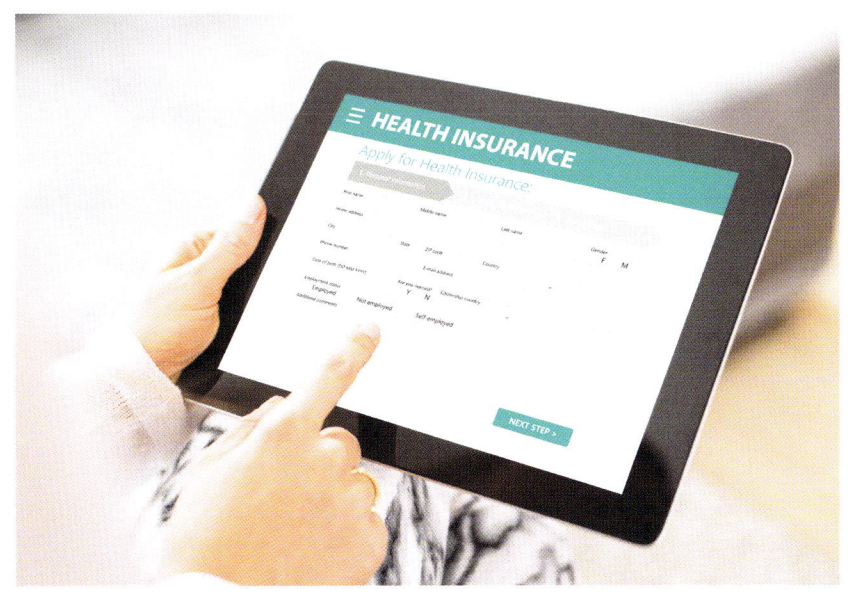

The increased use of electronic medical records has made the health-care industry a prime target for cyberattackers.

Jobs in Internet Security

Despite these dangers, health-care organizations have been slow to secure their systems—in part because many of these systems are old and outdated. This helps explain why health-care organizations experienced more than 1,300 security breaches between 2009 and 2015, exposing more than 150 million electronic health records to hackers. That's almost half the population of the United States! Pressure to protect private patient information (as well as the health of their patients) will no doubt drive health-care organizations to adapt—and fast. That means hiring coders who specialize in internet security to develop ways to protect health-care systems.

In addition to stepping up strikes against health-care organizations, hackers have increased attacks against manufacturing facilities. In fact, manufacturing is the second-most targeted industry among hackers. An attack against a manufacturing facility might not give someone access to much private information for use by identity thieves. However, it could result in the theft of trade secrets or intellectual property, like blueprints (which hackers could sell to the manufacturer's competitors or use to create knockoffs) or other sensitive information. It could also wreak havoc on any computerized machines that manufacture merchandise. For example, an attack could cause the machines to shut down or result in the production of defective or even dangerous products. This could lead to costly recalls—not to mention ruined reputations. Such an attack could even cause injuries or deaths—for example, if a computerized manufacturing machine were to explode or produce a faulty product that resulted in the user's injury or death. No manufacturer can afford such attacks, meaning they'll need to hire cybersecurity professionals to prevent them.

Online retail stores and banks are two other top targets for hackers—and have been since the early days of the internet. There are obvious reasons for this: these types of

Many manufacturing plants rely on computers to operate—making them potential targets for cyberattacks.

firms maintain extensive databases with private customer data and information about financial transactions. Not surprisingly, most of these organizations are further along in their efforts to secure themselves against hackers. Still, they have a continuing need for cybersecurity professionals on their staff.

These are not the only industries at risk of cyberattack and in need of coders who specialize in internet security. In truth, all industries are at risk. But these industries are among the most commonly targeted by hackers. As such, they are the most attractive industries for cybersecurity professionals.

Many schools, community colleges, and universities offer classes in computer coding. This man is learning how to code in his college class.

Coding Careers in Internet Security

chapter_05

Getting Involved

The shortage of computer coders means that people with coding skills are in great demand. This is particularly true of coders who specialize in internet security. There are far more jobs in this field than there are qualified people to fill them.

WHERE TO START

If you're interested in working as a coder in internet security, you should start preparing yourself now for that role. Fortunately, there are several resources available to help with this. These include online tools to learn how to code (some especially for girls), computer science classes for middle school and high school kids, and summer camps for coders.

After high school, you can complete college coursework to better your chances of landing a job as a computer coder who specializes in internet security. You can also obtain professional certifications.

ONLINE CODING RESOURCES

To work as a coder in internet security, you must first know how to code. There are lots of online instructional resources for kids who want to learn how to code. Here are just a few of them:

- Code Avengers (https://www.codeavengers.com): Code Avengers provides robust coding instruction—including courses in computer languages like HTML, JavaScript, and Python. Some courses are free; others require a paid subscription.

- Codecademy (https://www.codecademy.com): Codecademy offers several online coding tutorials with easy-to-follow instructions and immediate feedback. Like Code Avengers, Codecademy offers some courses free of charge and others through a paid subscription.

- Code.org (https://code.org): Code.org is a nonprofit whose mission is to give every student in every school the chance to explore computer science—the same way they do subjects like biology, chemistry, or algebra. To achieve this,

Code.org develops coursework for schools to use and offers free online coding courses and projects.

- Khan Academy (https://www.khanacademy.org/computing/computer-programming): Khan Academy's mission is "to provide a free, world-class education to anyone, anywhere." As part of this mission, it offers free classes on computer coding, including languages like JavaScript and HTML.

- Scratch (https://scratch.mit.edu): Offered by the Massachusetts Institute of Technology (MIT) Media Lab, Scratch provides tons of free tutorials and projects to teach coding concepts to kids, ages eight to sixteen.

- Tynker (https://www.tynker.com): Tynker offers self-paced, hands-on, online courses for kids to learn coding at home. Kids start by playing with visual code blocks that represent key programming concepts, and progress to programming languages like JavaScript and Python.

CODING RESOURCES FOR GIRLS

Research shows that 75 percent of high school girls are interested in STEM fields, including coding. However, just 0.4 percent of female college freshman say they plan to major in computer science. During the 2010s, several organizations formed to encourage more girls and women to become coders. Here are a few examples:

- Girls Who Code (https://girlswhocode.com): The mission of Girls Who Code is to close the gender gap in technology. To achieve this, the organization has taught basic coding skills to more than ninety thousand girls across the United States. "We're building the largest pipeline of future female engineers in the United States," says Reshma Saujani, who founded the organization in 2012. Apparently, the organization's methods are effective, as it is "on track to achieve gender parity in computer science by 2027," Saujani reports.

- Made with Code (https://www.madewithcode.com): Made with Code was launched by Google in 2014. It combines online activities with real-world events to encourage girls to learn to code. The site also features interviews with women whose careers involve coding.

- Black Girls Code (http://www.blackgirlscode.com): Girls and women are underrepresented in careers that involve coding—and African American girls and women are even more so. To change this, an African American electrical engineer named Kimberly Bryant founded Black Girls Code in 2011. The organization's mission is to "prove to the world that girls of every color have the skills to become the programmers of tomorrow" and to "train 1 million girls by 2040."

CODING CLASSES IN MIDDLE SCHOOLS AND HIGH SCHOOLS

Experts predict that computing jobs will be among the highest-paying jobs in coming years. Yet a 2016 survey by Google showed that just one in four schools teaches classes in computer programming. Even if a school does offer such classes, they might not count toward a student's graduation requirements. This discourages many students from taking them. Nonetheless, if you're interested in a career as a coder specializing in internet security, you should explore related course offerings at your school.

Reshma Saujani is the founder of Girls Who Code.

A young student practices her coding skills at school.

If no courses are offered, consider meeting with school administrators to suggest ways to add them—for example, partnering with a nonprofit coding organization like Code.org. Code.org offers free coding resources for schools, including curricula for grades K–12, workshops for teachers, and more. (For more information, see https://code.org/yourschool.) You could also start a computer coding club or a similar organization.

Taking instructor-guided coding classes outside school—either online or in person—is another option. For example, organizations like Code Wizards HQ and Coding with Kids offer online teacher-led classes. Establishments like Sylvan Learning and theCoderSchool offer after-school classes.

CODING CAMP

Various organizations offer summer camps to teach kids about coding. For example, the NSA and the National Science Foundation (NSF) have teamed up since 2014 to offer a series of summer day camps called the NSA GenCyber camps. These camps are for kids grades K–12 who are interested in coding in general and in cybersecurity in particular. They are offered at several sites throughout the country and are open to all participants free of charge. (For more information, see https://www.gen-cyber.com.) Other organizations that offer day camps for coders—although not for free—include Codeverse and iD Tech.

Black Girls Code is devoted to training one million young black girls to code by 2040.

Getting Involved [63]

COLLEGE COURSEWORK AND MOOCS FOR CYBERSECURITY SPECIALISTS

Cybersecurity jobs do not necessarily require a college degree. It's possible to acquire the skills for these jobs in other ways—for example, online, at a community college, or in the military. However, people who earn college degrees in computer science will have more opportunity for higher-paying jobs in cybersecurity from the beginning.

To help college students prepare for a career in cybersecurity, the NSA has developed a special program that has been adopted by several universities nationwide. It is called the National Centers of Academic Excellence in Cyber Operations (CAE-CO) program. According to the NSA, this program "is a deeply technical, inter-disciplinary, higher

The GenCyber Camp, offered by the NSA and the NSF, provides free training for kids who are interested in coding.

Coding Careers in Internet Security

education program" that provides "a particular emphasis on technologies and techniques related to specialized cyber operations."

Students who enter a CAE-CO program (or equivalent) might be eligible for a scholarship from the National Science Foundation in conjunction with the US Department of Homeland Security. This scholarship is called the Scholarship for Service. It gives qualified students a stipend, or set amount of pay, of up to $20,000 per year for undergraduate studies. (Scholarships for graduate and doctoral studies are also available.) In return, students must accept a government position in the area of cybersecurity—for example, at the NSA or CIA—for a set period of time after their schooling is complete.

Some universities and other educational institutions offer classes in computer science even for people who aren't enrolled. These are called massive online open courses (MOOCs). These courses are usually free and are often taught by top professors. Here are a few popular MOOCs worth checking out:

- **Future Learn Introduction to Cybersecurity**
- **Massachusetts Institute of Technology Introduction to Computer Science and Programming**
- **Springboard Foundations of Cybersecurity**

NASA'S CYBERSECURITY AND PRIVACY DIVISION

NASA has its own cybersecurity division. They help keep company computers and projects safe, including those in the flight control room, shown here.

No organization is safe from the dangers of malware and hackers—not even ones that operate in space! The US National Aeronautics and Space Administration (NASA) found this out the hard way in 2012 when hackers in China broke into their systems and accessed sensitive files. This breach caused members of the US Congressional Committee on Science, Space, and Technology to observe that "the threat to NASA's information security is persistent and ever changing. Unless NASA is able to continuously innovate and adapt, their data, systems, and operations will continue to be endangered."

To secure its systems from outside attack by hackers and other malicious types, NASA formed the Cybersecurity & Privacy Division (CSPD). Coders and other cybersecurity specialists in this division run penetration tests to check NASA systems for vulnerabilities and perform other important security-related tasks. The cyber professionals who work in the CSPD don't just ensure the safety of critical computer systems—some of which cost millions of taxpayer dollars to build. They also guarantee that blueprints for space shuttles and other technologies don't fall into the wrong hands—not to mention keeping astronauts who rely on these systems during training and space travel safe.

CYBERSECURITY CERTIFICATIONS

Aspiring cybersecurity professionals can earn various professional certifications or credentials. These offer proof to potential employers that the professional knows their stuff. Obtaining certifications or credentials usually involves taking a class and/or passing an exam.

There are several certifying organizations. One of these is called Global Information Assurance Certification (GIAC). This organization was formed in 1999 to validate the skills of security professionals. GIAC offers certification in such cybersecurity specialties as incident handler, forensic examiner, penetration tester, and reverse engineering malware.

Whether you're interested in building malware or securing systems against threats, in attending college or learning how to code in some other way, one thing is clear: for young people interested in pursuing a career in cybersecurity, the sky is the limit!

Glossary

algorithm A well-defined procedure that enables a computer to complete a task or solve a problem.

anti-malware A computer program that prevents a malware program from penetrating a computer system and that scans computer systems to detect and delete any malware that sneaks through.

artificial intelligence (AI) The science and engineering behind "intelligent" machines.

bug An error or flaw in a computer system or program (usually in its source code) that causes it to behave in an unintended way. Bugs often open a pathway for malware to exploit the system.

cipher A secret way of writing, such as a code.

cloud computing Using computers on the internet to run software or services rather than using one's own "local" computer.

emulator A virtual computer environment that operates within a regular computer environment but is isolated from other resources.

encryption Using a code to make data unreadable.

ethical hacking Breaking into a computer system the same way a hacker does to help an organization identify security flaws in its computer systems.

generic decryption A malware-detection mechanism that loads all new program files into an emulator to scan for malware.

hacker Someone who creates malware or uses a computer to gain unauthorized access to data.

identity theft The act of stealing personal data and using it to fraudulently apply for credit cards or loans.

Internet of Things A network of everyday devices and appliances that are connected to the internet.

machine language Language that a computer can read. Machine language consists of a series of zeroes and ones. The order in which these zeroes and ones appear dictates how the program will behave.

machine learning (ML) The ability of machines to learn through experience over time.

machine learning model An algorithm that is designed to enable a machine to "learn" from experience over time.

malware A type of computer program built by hackers to damage or exploit a computer system in some way.

nonprofit An organization that does not make a profit. An example of a nonprofit is a charity.

object code Code that contains program instructions in machine language.

open security A security strategy that uses open source software.

open source Software whose source code is available to the general public to study or even modify.

patch A piece of code meant to fix a security flaw in an operating system or computer program.

phishing Sending email messages that warn users of some type of problem and instruct them to click a link in the message to find out more. When the user clicks the link, they download a Trojan horse onto their machine.

sandbox An isolated virtual space for testing software.

self-replication Describes when a virus or worm makes a copy of itself.

signature A string of bits in a piece of code that acts like a fingerprint to identify the code.

source code Code that contains program instructions in a programming language.

STEM Short for science, technology, engineering, and math. Often used to describe educational programs in one or all of these areas.

Trojan horse A type of malware that hackers spread by tricking users into installing it.

virus A type of malware that spreads by self-replicating and attaching copies of itself to other programs or files.

worm A type of malware that spreads by self-replicating. Unlike a virus, a worm doesn't need to attach itself to a program or file to spread. It can spread all on its own.

Further Information

BOOKS

Briggs, Jason R. Python for Kids: *A Playful Introduction to Programming*. San Francisco, CA: No Starch Press, 2012.

McCue, Camille. *Coding for Kids*. 2nd edition. For Dummies. Hoboken, NJ: John Wiley & Sons, 2019.

Minnick, Chris, and Eva Holland. *JavaScript for Kids*. For Dummies. Hoboken, NJ: John Wiley & Sons, 2015.

Sande, Warren, and Carter Sande. *Hello World!: Computer Programming for Kids and Other Beginners*. 2nd edition. Shelter Island, NY: Manning Publications, 2013.

Saujani, Reshma. *Girls Who Code: Learn to Code and Change the World*. New York: Viking Books for Young Readers, 2017.

WEBSITES

CERT
https://www.us-cert.gov
Keep track of emerging cyber threats and other cybersecurity news on this site.

CYBER DEGREES
https://www.cyberdegrees.org
This site offers a comprehensive directory of career paths, free online security courses, and more.

WIRED THREAT LEVEL

https://www.wired.com/category/threatlevel

For informative news stories on security issues, check out *Wired* magazine's Threat Level page.

MUSEUMS AND ORGANIZATIONS

THE NATIONAL CRYPTOLOGIC MUSEUM

https://www.nsa.gov/about/cryptologic-heritage/museum

This museum offers a peek into the secret world of code making and code breaking.

NATIONAL SECURITY AGENCY (NSA)

https://www.nsa.gov

This is the top organization responsible for cybersecurity throughout the United States.

THE OPEN WEB APPLICATION SECURITY PROJECT (OWASP)

https://www.owasp.org/index.php/Main_Page

This nonprofit organization is focused on improving security through open source software.

Selected Bibliography

Ablon, Lillian. *Data Thieves: The Motivations of Cyber Threat Actors and Their Use and Monetization of Stolen Data.* Rand Corporation, March 15, 2018. Accessed December 8, 2018. https://www.rand.org/content/dam/rand/pubs/testimonies/CT400/CT490/RAND_CT490.pdf.

Carbon Black. "The Ransomware Economy." October 2017. Accessed December 3, 2018. https://www.carbonblack.com/wp-content/uploads/2017/10/Carbon-Black-Ransomware-Economy-Report-101117.pdf.

Cohen, Fred. "Computer Viruses: Theory and Experiments." *Computers and Security* 6 (1987): 22–35.

"Computer Viruses and Malware Facts & FAQs." Kaspersky Lab. Accessed December 8, 2018. https://usa.kaspersky.com/resource-center/threats/computer-viruses-and-malware-facts-and-faqs.

Fisk, Dale. *Programming with Punched Cards.* 2005. Accessed November 29, 2018. http://www.columbia.edu/cu/computinghistory/fisk.pdf.

Glaser, April. "Encryption Pioneers Win Computing's Most Prestigious Award." *Wired*, March 2, 2016. https://www.wired.com/2016/03/encryption-pioneers-win-computings-prestigious-award.

Gookin, Dan. "Know the Different Types of Malware". Dummies. Accessed December 8, 2018. https://www.dummies.com/computers/pcs/know-the-different-types-of-malware.

Greenberg, Andy. "The Untold Story of NotPetya, the Most Devastating Cyberattack in History." *Wired*, August 22, 2018. https://www.wired.com/story/notpetya-cyberattack-ukraine-russia-code-crashed-the-world.

"How Coding Works." Code Conquest. Accessed November 29, 2018. https://www.codeconquest.com/what-is-coding/how-does-coding-work.

"How the Internet Was Born: From the ARPANET to the Internet." The Conversation. November 2, 2016. https://theconversation.com/how-the-internet-was-born-from-the-arpanet-to-the-internet-68072.

The "I Love You" Computer Virus and the Financial Services Industry. Before the Subcommittee on Financial Institutions of the Committee on Banking, Housing, and Urban Affairs, U.S. Senate. (May 18, 2000) (testimony of Stephen R. Malphus, Staff Director for Management). https://www.federalreserve.gov/boarddocs/testimony/2000/20000518.htm#fn4.

"Jobs in Cyber Security." Cyber Degrees. Accessed December 6, 2018. https://www.cyberdegrees.org/jobs.

Keeney, Kevin. "Why Open-Sourced Code Can Boost Cybersecurity." The Fifth Domain. August 16, 2018. https://www.fifthdomain.com/thought-leadership/2018/08/16/why-open-sourced-code-can-boost-cybersecurity.

Keilman, John. "Coding Education Rare in K-12 Schools But Starting to Catch On." *Chicago Tribune*, January 2, 2016. https://www.chicagotribune.com/news/ct-coding-high-school-met-20160101-story.html.

Landesman, Mary. "A Brief History of Malware." Lifewire. September 2, 2018. Accessed December 8, 2018. https://www.lifewire.com/brief-history-of-malware-153616.

Libicki, Martin C., David Senty, and Julia Pollak. H4CKER5 WANTED: *An Examination of the Cybersecurity Labor Market*. Rand Corporation, 2014. Accessed December 6, 2018. https://www.rand.org/content/dam/rand/pubs/research_reports/RR400/RR430/RAND_RR430.pdf.

"Machine Learning: What It Is and Why It Matters." SAS. Accessed December 8, 2018. https://www.sas.com/en_us/insights/analytics/machine-learning.html.

Malanov, Alexey. "Antivirus Fundamentals: Viruses, Signatures, Disinfection." Kaspersky Lab. October 13, 2016. https://www.kaspersky.com/blog/signature-virus-disinfection/13233.

Meyer, David. "Russia Blamed for 'Costliest Cyberattack in History': What You Need to Know." *Fortune*, February 16, 2016.

http://fortune.com/2018/02/16/russia-notpetya-cyberattack-damage.

Nakashima, Ellen. "Powerful NSA Hacking Tools Have Been Revealed Online." *Washington Post*, August 16, 2016. https://www.washingtonpost.com/world/national-security/powerful-nsa-hacking-tools-have-been-revealed-online/2016/08/16/bce4f974-63c7-11e6-96c0-37533479f3f5_story.html?utm_term=.16b6d7d8df5b.

"The 100 Best Jobs." *US News & World Report*, January 10, 2018. https://money.usnews.com/careers/best-jobs/rankings/the-100-best-jobs.

Rampell, Catherine. "I Am Woman, Watch Me Hack." *New York Times Magazine*, October 22, 2013, p.14.

Rothman, Lily. "Remember Y2K? Here's How We Prepped for the Non-Disaster." *Time*, December 31, 2014. http://time.com/3645828/y2k-look-back.

Schiffman, Mike. "A Brief History of Malware Obfuscation: Part 1 of 2." February 15, 2010. Cisco Blog. Accessed December 8, 2018. https://blogs.cisco.com/security/a_brief_history_of_malware_obfuscation_part_1_of_2.

"Understanding the Threat." NSA | CSS. Accessed December 6, 2018. https://www.nsa.gov/what-we-do/understanding-the-threat.

Index

Page numbers in **boldface** refer to images.

algorithm, 22, 31, 34
Amazon, 26, **27**, 36, **37**
anti-malware, 12, **14**, 17, 25, **28**, 35, 40–41
   generic decryption, 33
   next-generation methods, 33–34
   traditional strategies, 31–32
ARPANET, 7, 18–19
artificial intelligence (AI), 36

bugs, 16–17, 23–24, 48

Central Intelligence Agency (CIA) 13, 49, 65
cipher, 12, 52
Clinton, Bill, **24**
cloud computing, 28, 34, 36
code, **6**, 12, 52
   encrypted, 32
   interpreted, 35
   metamorphic, 32, 34
   object code, 35
   oligomorphic, 32
   open source code, 39–40
   patch, 21
   polymorphic, 32
   source code, 6, 17, 35, 38, 48
coder groups, 25, 28

coding
   history, 5–6
   in internet security, 7–9
   languages, 35, 38
   process, 6
crypto currency, 22–23
cyber warfare, 21, 52

dark web, 22, 29
Diffie, Whitfield, 10–11, **10**

education, coding, 57–58
   camps, 63
   certification, 68
   colleges, 64–65
   for girls, 59–60
   MOOCs, 65
   online resources, 58–59
   scholarships, 65
   school resources, 61–62
employment opportunities, 9, 12–13, 45–48
   banking, 54–55
   government, 46–47, 49–50, 52
   health-care, 50–51, 53
   manufacturing, 53–54, **54**
   retail, 54–55
   salaries, 45
emulator, 33–34, 36
encryption, 10–11
ethical hacking, 13

Federal Bureau of Investigation (FBI), 29, 41, 49
  computer forensic lab, **42**

hackers, 10, 12–13, 15–17, 27–29, 41–43, 46–47, 50–51, 53–55, 66–67
  definition, 8–9
  encryption, 32
  history, 17–20
  machine learning, 34
  modern attacks, 20–23
  white-hat hackers, 13
Hellman, Martin, 10–11, **10**

identity theft, 8
Internet of Things, 28
internet security (cybersecurity), 7–9, 28–29
  anti-malware, 12
  companies, 25
  in e-commerce, 26–27
  in European Union (EU), 43
  government efforts, 41–43, 66–67
  history, 24–25, 28
  legislation, 41–42

Kaspersky Lab, 17, 25, 46

machine language, 35
machine learning (ML), 34, 36–37
machine learning model, 34

malware, 9, 12, 15–17, 25, 28–29, 31–37, 46, 52, 66, 68
  history, 17–20
  modern attacks, 20–23
  Trojan horse, 17, 19
  viruses, 16, 19–20, 25, 31
  worms, 16, 18, 25, 52
Morris, Robert, 18, **18**

National Aeronautics and Space Administration (NASA)
  cybersecurity division, 66–67, **66**
National Science Foundation (NSF), 63, 65
National Security Agency (NSA), 7–8, 11, 13, 22, 49, 52, 63–65
nonprofit, 40, 58, 62

object code, 35
open security, 40
open source, 39–40

Pentagon, **8**
phishing, 17
punch cards **4**, 5–6

sandbox, 34
Saujani, Reshma, 60, **61**
self-replication, 16, 18–19
signature, 31–33, 36
STEM, 59

Index [79]

About the Author

Kate Shoup has written more than forty books and has edited hundreds more. When not working, Shoup loves to travel, watch Indy car racing, ski, read, and ride her motorcycle. She lives in Indianapolis with her husband.